Especially for

From

Date

THE BIBLE PROMISE BOOK®

for Women

PRAYER EDITION JOURNAL

ISBN 978-1-63409-075-9

Chapter introductions written by Tina Krause.

Prayers are taken from *Prayers from the Heart*, published by Barbour Publishing, Inc.

Published by Barbour Books, an imprint of Barbour Publishing, Inc., P.O. Box 719, Uhrichsville, Ohio 44683, www.barbourbooks.com

Our mission is to publish and distribute inspirational products offering exceptional value and biblical encouragement to the masses.

ecpa Member of the Evangelical Christian Publishers Association

Printed in China.

THE BIBLE PROMISE BOOK® *for Women*

Prayer Edition Journal

BARBOUR BOOKS
An Imprint of Barbour Publishing, Inc.

Adversity

No one is exempt from problems. From the palace to the poorhouse, women throughout the ages have fought and conquered adversity in their lives.

Queen Esther risked losing her only relative and her people. Using her influence, she saved the Israelites from destruction. Interestingly, the Jewish name *Esther* means "Hadassah," which comes from the word *myrtle*—the tree whose leaves only release fragrance when they are crushed.

Are you facing adversity? Perhaps your faith has brought reproach or daily struggles have robbed your faith. Regardless, the scriptures ease the crush of adversity, releasing the sweet fragrance of God's overcoming power.

For I reckon that the sufferings of this present time are not worthy to be compared with the glory which shall be revealed in us.

ROMANS 8:18 KJV

Lord, I know I can't hope to escape every unpleasant circumstance in this world. Just the same, I will trust in You, whatever comes. Protect me in the way You see fit, in the way that best advances Your purpose for my life. Amen.

"These things I have spoken to you, that in Me you may have peace. In the world you will have tribulation; but be of good cheer, I have overcome the world."

John 16:33 NKJV

In the midst of suffering,
I want to keep my eyes on You,
Jesus. The suffering You endured
for my sake makes my trials look
like nothing. Help me look forward
to the promise and to forget the
temporary troubles I have now.
Amen.

Are any of you suffering hardships? You should pray.
JAMES 5:13 NLT

Lord, I know bad things will come my way in life, but I am secure in Your love that never fails. I am constantly blessed by Your care and concern. I am so important to You that even the hairs of my head are all numbered. Amen.

Dear friends, do not be surprised at the painful trial you are suffering, as though something strange were happening to you. But rejoice inasmuch as you participate in the sufferings of Christ, so that you may be overjoyed when his glory is revealed.

1 PETER 4:12–13 NIV

Our Creator never intended that we should shoulder a load of suffering ourselves. That's the whole purpose of spiritual community.

LINDA BARTLETT

Anger

It doesn't matter who was right or wrong. You *feel* wronged and anger simmers on the verge of full boil.

Can we be angry and not sin? To feel anger is one thing, to act on it is another. When we use our anger to justify our wrongful deeds, we sin.

The Bible, however, gives us clear and concise instructions on how to handle anger or angry people. How can we curb anger, irritations, and flare-ups? Apply the calming influence of God's Word to our circumstance. Ah, yes. That's better.

So then, my beloved brethren, let every man be swift to hear, slow to speak, slow to wrath; for the wrath of man does not produce the righteousness of God.

JAMES 1:19–20 NKJV

Lord, help me be the peacekeeper, never the one who stirs up more anger. Help me be an example to my whole family. Amen.

Be not hasty in thy spirit to be angry:
for anger resteth in the bosom of fools.
ECCLESIASTES 7:9 KJV

Today in anger, I said something I shouldn't have. Forgive me, Lord. Instead of speaking in anger and frustration, I want to fill my mouth with words of continual praise to You. Amen.

"But I tell you that anyone who is angry with his brother or sister will be subject to judgment. Again, anyone who says to his brother or sister, 'Raca,' is answerable to the court. But anyone who says, 'You fool!' will be in danger of the fire of hell."

MATTHEW 5:22 NIV

Lord, in the heat of anger, control my tongue, because what I say then can be as damaging to my soul as it is to my victim's reputation. Amen.

"In your anger do not sin": Do not let the sun go down while you are still angry.

EPHESIANS 4:26 NIV

Being angry or unforgiving makes it impossible to have a gentle and quiet spirit.

DARLENE WILKINSON

Comfort

A loved one passes away, and friends and family surround you with prayers and comforting words. Illness strikes a blow, but friends support and comfort you. Problems weigh heavy and there seems no way out, but the scriptures speak comfort to your heart.

Moms comfort their sick children with hugs and chicken soup. Similarly, God eases our pain and lightens our load through the comfort of His Word and His Spirit. Jesus called the Holy Spirit "the Comforter." He is the One who teaches, guides, soothes, and stands with us. The Comforter comforts like no one else can.

Blessed be the God and Father of our Lord Jesus Christ, the Father of mercies and God of all comfort, who comforts us in all our tribulation, that we may be able to comfort those who are in any trouble, with the comfort with which we ourselves are comforted by God.

2 CORINTHIANS 1:3–4 NKJV

Lord, remove the fears that bind me so that I can be happy in the knowledge that You are there to comfort me—no matter what else is happening. Amen.

Even when I walk through the darkest valley,
I will not be afraid, for you are close beside me.
Your rod and your staff protect and comfort me.
PSALM 23:4 NLT

Lord, life seems overwhelming to me sometimes. Please give me the abundant wisdom You've promised and help me to relax in the knowledge that You will guide me. Amen.

Praise be to the God and Father of our Lord Jesus Christ, the Father of compassion and the God of all comfort, who comforts us in all our troubles, so that we can comfort those in any trouble with the comfort we ourselves receive from God. For just as we share abundantly in the suffering of Christ, so also our comfort abounds through Christ.

2 Corinthians 1:3–5 NIV

Father, my trials are not major, so far. But I know that things can go wrong in an instant. When I cry to You, I know You hear. Thank You for Your promises and never-ending care. Amen.

Finally, brethren, farewell. Become complete.
Be of good comfort, be of one mind, live in peace;
and the God of love and peace will be with you.
2 CORINTHIANS 13:11 NKJV

All you really need is the One who promised never to leave or forsake you—the One who said, "Lo, I am with you always."
JONI EARECKSON TADA

Conversation

Have you ever blurted out the wrong words at the wrong time? Mortified, you wish you could push rewind and start again—but unfortunately, the words are irretrievable.

The scriptures tell us to keep watch over our tongue, and for good reason. Words have the power to create strife or peace; to uplift or destroy; to bless or to curse.

The old adage claims "words will never hurt me." That, however, is untrue. Wrong words *do* hurt, but the right words spoken at the right time have the power to heal and comfort. Words count—so count your words!

The heart of the righteous studieth to answer:
but the mouth of the wicked poureth out evil things.
PROVERBS 15:28 KJV

O God, help me think before I speak. Put words of kindness in my mouth that will build up others instead of destroying them. I desire to be virtuous. Amen.

The hearts of the wise make their mouths prudent, and their lips promote instruction. Gracious words are a honeycomb, sweet to the soul and healing to the bones.

Proverbs 16:23–24 NIV

Lord, help my words to be blessings to those around me in my daily life. Amen.

There is one who speaks rashly like the thrusts of a sword,
but the tongue of the wise brings healing.
PROVERBS 12:18 NASB

Lord, the next time I am angry, guide me away from sin until I can speak words of peace and comfort once again. Amen.

A man has joy by the answer of his mouth,
and a word spoken in due season, how good it is!
PROVERBS 15:23 NKJV

Kind words can be short and easy to speak, but their echoes are truly endless.
MOTHER TERESA

Counsel

Were you ever so immersed in a problem that you felt like you were drowning? Have you ever had to make a decision and didn't know what to do? At those times we turn to God—often through godly counsel, perhaps from a pastor or trusted Christian friend.

We all need counsel and direction sometimes. The old saying that "two heads are better than one" is not only noteworthy, it's scriptural!

King Solomon said that to seek godly counsel is wise. Moreover, to grow spiritually we must maintain an open, teachable spirit.

Good advice comes from God-advice. Now that's good counsel.

Get all the advice and instruction you can,
so you will be wise the rest of your life.
PROVERBS 19:20 NLT

Lord, if there's one thing I need, it's trustworthy guidance. In darkness or light, on fair days or foul, I trust that the light of Your Word will bring me safely home. Amen.

"All your children will be taught by the LORD, and great will be their peace."

ISAIAH 54:13 NIV

Lord, guard my tongue as I teach my children. Season my speech with grace–to encourage my children and remind them to walk in Your path. Amen.

"Because the Lord disciplines the one he loves, and he chastens everyone he accepts as his son. Endure hardship as discipline; God is treating you as his children. For what children are not disciplined by their father?"

HEBREWS 12:6–7 NIV

Lord, show me my errors and teach me the proper way to take advice. Amen.

For a child will be born to us, a son will be given to us; and the government will rest on His shoulders; and His name will be called Wonderful Counselor, Mighty God, Eternal Father, Prince of Peace.
ISAIAH 9:6 NASB

The true secret of giving advice is, after you have honestly given it, to be perfectly indifferent whether it is taken or not, and never persist in trying to set people right.
HANNAH WHITALL SMITH

Courage

Few of us require the kind of courage that Daniel had when he entered the lions' den or that David exercised when he confronted the giant. Nevertheless, courage is needed to conquer our fears, proclaim our faith, and overcome adversity. Oftentimes, we need courage just to get through the day!

The following verses provide instructions and admonitions to build our faith and fortitude. They equip us with the courage we need to conquer our giants in life's den of lions.

Wait on the LORD: be of good courage, and he shall strengthen thine heart: wait, I say, on the LORD.

PSALM 27:14 KJV

Lord, when it comes to courage, I have none of my own. Without You, I would be filled with fear, terrified of a future I cannot see. Thank You for patiently taking my hand and helping me face my fears. Amen.

The wicked flee though no one pursues,
but the righteous are as bold as a lion.
PROVERBS 28:1 NIV

Lord, I've often found myself afraid. Please help me remember where my strength and salvation come from and to say with confidence, "Whom shall I fear? Of whom shall I be afraid?" Amen.

Therefore, brethren, having boldness to enter the Holiest by the blood of Jesus, by a new and living way which He consecrated for us, through the veil, that is, His flesh, and having a High Priest over the house of God, let us draw near with a true heart in full assurance of faith.

HEBREWS 10:19–22 NKJV

Lord, please increase my inner strength. Remind me that although I seem powerless, Your power knows no limits and You will provide whatever strength I need to see me through my current crisis. Amen.

So be strong and courageous,
all you who put your hope in the LORD!
PSALM 31:24 NLT

You have to accept whatever comes and the only important thing is that you meet it with courage, and with the best you have to give.
ELEANOR ROOSEVELT

Diligence

The author of Ecclesiastes wrote: "Whatever your hand finds to do, do it with all your might." Diligence keeps going while frustration gives up. Diligence acts while procrastination rests. Diligence says, "I can do it" while defeat says, "I can't."

To work with diligence is essential to every facet of our spiritual and physical lives. With devoted tenacity we seek God and His will. With steadfast determination, we pray and study His Word.

Wherever we are or whatever we do, God calls us to remain diligent—even when our greatest efforts seem vain or our hard work goes unnoticed.

"But be very careful to keep the commandment and the law that Moses the servant of the Lord gave you: to love the Lord your God, to walk in obedience to him, to keep his commands, to hold fast to him and to serve him with all your heart and with all your soul."

JOSHUA 22:5 NIV

Lord, I often make mistakes on the path of life, losing sight of the trail and calling out for You. Thank You for finding me, for putting my feet back on the path and leading me home. Amen.

Therefore, my dear brothers and sisters stand firm. Let nothing move you. Always give yourselves fully to the work of the Lord, because you know that your labor in the Lord is not in vain.
1 CORINTHIANS 15:58 NIV

Father, I don't know how You will use my life, but I have faith in Your promises and am always ready to do Your will. Amen.

So let's not get tired of doing what is good. At just the right time we will reap a harvest of blessing if we don't give up.

Galatians 6:9 NLT

Lord, show me the path to victory every day, because sometimes I find it hard to follow. You know every turn in the road, and I will follow You in security all the days of my life. Amen.

Whatever your hand finds to do,
do it with all your might.
ECCLESIASTES 9:10 NASB

When I stand before God
at the end of my life,
I would hope that I would
not have a single bit of
talent left, and could say,
"I used everything you gave me."
ERMA BOMBECK

God's Discipline

Ouch! Did you ever feel like God dispensed a spiritual spanking? Just as we discipline our children, our heavenly Father disciplines us. Why? Because an undisciplined life brings bondage while a disciplined life liberates. Yes, discipline frees us.

The Lord has a good reason for everything He does, and everything He does comes from love. So rather than bemoaning the temporary pain, consider discipline's benefits: It teaches, guides, garners appreciation, gives life, establishes our spiritual "daughtership," and yields the peaceable fruit of righteousness within us.

Admit it. Discipline helps way more than it hurts!

And you have forgotten the exhortation which is addressed to you as sons, "MY SON, DO NOT REGARD LIGHTLY THE DISCIPLINE OF THE LORD, NOR FAINT WHEN YOU ARE REPROVED BY HIM; FOR THOSE WHOM THE LORD LOVES HE DISCIPLINES, AND HE SCOURGES EVERY SON WHOM HE RECEIVES." It is for discipline that you endure; God deals with you as with sons; for what son is there whom his father does not discipline? But if you are without discipline, of which all have become partakers, then you are illegitimate children and not sons.

HEBREWS 12:5–8 NASB

Father, Your correction lasts only a moment; but its blessings are eternal. When I realize You are so concerned for me and want to help me, I am filled with gratitude and willing to be led in the right direction. Amen.

Know then in your heart that as a man disciplines his son, so the LORD your God disciplines you.

DEUTERONOMY 8:5 NIV

Father, I need to show my children how important obedience is by being obedient myself—to You and to others in authority over me. Thank You for assisting me in this effort. Amen.

For whom the LORD loves He corrects,
just as a father the son in whom he delights.
PROVERBS 3:12 NKJV

Father, help me see when my children need gentle, loving correction, and show me the best approach. Let me be as kind and patient with my children as You are with me. Amen.

"I correct and discipline everyone I love.
So be diligent and turn from your indifference."
REVELATION 3:19 NLT

God has to punish His children from time to time and it is the very demonstration of His love.
ELISABETH ELLIOT

Duty

What is a Christian woman's duty? The scriptures list a few: to revere, serve, and obey God and keep His commandments.

In the 1940s and '50s a married woman's "duty" was clearly defined—to love and respect her husband while caring for her home and children. Today society has changed. God's Word, however, remains the same.

Our duty to love and respect our husbands, and care for our homes and children comes from our desire to follow biblical precepts. When we obey God and keep His commands, we automatically gain a sense of servitude toward our family and others.

What's our duty? To love God and follow His will.

Let us hear the conclusion of the whole matter: Fear God, and keep his commandments: for this is the whole duty of man.

ECCLESIASTES 12:13 KJV

Through You, Lord, I can live a life that will give others no right to accuse me of any wrongdoing. I pray that You'll allow my life to be an example that will encourage my family, friends, and others to come to You. Amen.

"Be careful to listen to all these words which I command you, so that it may be well with you and your sons after you forever, for you will be doing what is good and right in the sight of the LORD your God."
DEUTERONOMY 12:28 NASB

Lord, make me a living sacrifice for You, that I might lead others to You. Let my praises be a godly example in my home. I praise You with all that is within me. Amen.

"Now if you obey me fully and keep my covenant, then out of all nations you will be my treasured possession. Although the whole earth is mine."

EXODUS 19:5 NIV

Father, my daily problems come and go; yet if I remain steadfast and dedicated, doing the work You have given me to do, I am confident that my reward awaits me. Thank You, Lord. Amen

"You shall therefore keep His statutes and His commandments which I command you today, that it may go well with you and with your children after you, and that you may prolong your days in the land which the LORD your God is giving you for all time."

DEUTERONOMY 4:40 NKJV

Laziness may appear attractive, but work gives satisfaction.

ANNE FRANK

Encouragement

A little encouragement goes a long way.

It's been a bad week. You lost your car keys, burned your favorite recipe, misplaced important papers, ran late for work, and forgot a parent-teacher conference. Plus, your devotional time seems to have disappeared with those keys.

Discouraged, you enter church on Sunday fully prepared to force a fake smile. Instead, you're encouraged. The Sunday school lesson and sermon are just for you and the fellowship is great. Instantly, your deflated optimism fades into the distant past and you are revitalized, ready to share the encouragement you received with someone else.

You must warn each other every day, while it is still "today," so that none of you will be deceived by sin and hardened against God.

HEBREWS 3:13 NLT

Lord, on days when I'm having spiritual struggles, my thoughts become full of discouragement and frustration. I don't like to be so controlled by my emotions. Please give me the strength to be pure in every situation. Amen.

All Scripture is God-breathed and is useful for teaching, rebuking, correcting and training in righteousness.

2 TIMOTHY 3:16 NIV

Lord, help me to teach my children that to grow as encouragers they can start with small things as they comfort others and build from there. Amen.

Not giving up meeting together, as some are in the habit of doing, but encouraging one another— and all the more as you see the Day approaching.

HEBREWS 10:25 NIV

Lord, You've given me a life that abounds with rich blessings, and You've guaranteed that because of this You also have great expectations of me. Help me to be faithful to these expectations. Amen.

Do not merely look out for your own personal interests, but also for the interests of others.

PHILIPPIANS 2:4 NASB

What men and women need is encouragement. . . .Instead of always harping on a man's faults, tell him of his virtues. Try to pull him out of his rut of bad habits.

ELEANOR H. PORTER

Eternity

Earthly life is short but eternity is forever. With that in mind, we all need to stand ready to meet the Lord. Heaven is an actual place, not some mystical golden-gated wisp of cumulus clouds topped with angels. The most majestic places, ideals, and valued treasures can't compare to what God has prepared for those who love Him. And the best part about heaven is the One who rules and reigns there.

Right now, Jesus prepares your eternal home. And one day all of life's problems and trials will vanish in the light of an eternity with Him.

"There is more than enough room in my Father's home. If this were not so, would I have told you that I am going to prepare a place for you? When everything is ready, I will come and get you, so that you will always be with me where I am."

JOHN 14:2–3 NLT

Forever, *Lord—what encouragement is in that word. We have all eternity to spend with You in heaven. Thank You for this indescribable gift. Thank You for being the Alpha and the Omega, the first and the last. Amen.*

"But don't be so concerned about perishable things like food. Spend your energy seeking the eternal life that the Son of Man can give you. For God the Father has given me the seal of his approval."

John 6:27 NLT

Lord, if I trust You for my eternal salvation, why don't I trust You for my daily needs? Instill in me the peace that comes from casting all my cares on You. Amen.

In the future there is laid up for me the crown of righteousness, which the Lord, the righteous Judge, will award to me on that day; and not only to me, but also to all who have loved His appearing.

2 TIMOTHY 4:8 NASB

Father, when my time on earth comes to an end, I pray I will be able to bear death as well as I bore life, secure in Your love and looking to the salvation that You have promised is mine. Amen.

Therefore are they before the throne of God, and serve him day and night in his temple: and he that sitteth on the throne shall dwell among them. They shall hunger no more, neither thirst any more; neither shall the sun light on them, nor any heat. For the Lamb which is in the midst of the throne shall feed them, and shall lead them unto living fountains of waters: and God shall wipe away all tears from their eyes.

REVELATION 7:15–17 KJV

Redeemed, how I love to proclaim it! His child, and forever, I am.

FANNIE CROSBY

Faith

You may be unaware of it, but you exercise faith daily. By faith you fall asleep, confident of morning. You eat, expecting nourishment. You breathe in air you can't see. You drive your car, trusting it will take you to your destination.

Jesus said that faith as tiny as a mustard seed is enough to produce miraculous results. So why do we assume that only mountain-moving faith will do? The Word of God is a faith-builder. So read on and cause that mustard seed to flourish and grow.

But he must ask in faith without any doubting, for the one who doubts is like the surf of the sea, driven and tossed by the wind.

JAMES 1:6 NASB

Lord, my faith seems weak—not the type of faith that might bring victory. But in You I have the assurance of victory. I've read the story, and in the end You will reign victorious. I praise You, Lord. Amen.

And now, just as you accepted Christ Jesus as your Lord, you must continue to follow him. Let your roots grow down into him, and let your lives be built on him. Then your faith will grow strong in the truth you were taught, and you will overflow with thankfulness.

Colossians 2:6–7 NLT

Lord, keep me strong in my faith, no matter what. When I am following You, I can be blessed, no matter what others say about me. Thank You, Jesus, for mapping the way for me. Amen.

And Jesus said to him, "'If You can?'
All things are possible to him who believes."
MARK 9:23 NASB

I often feel that I lack faith, Lord, that You must be speaking promises for someone else–someone more faithful and deserving of them. Show me the error of this thinking. Amen.

Let us draw near with a sincere heart in full assurance of faith, having our hearts sprinkled clean from an evil conscience and our bodies washed with pure water.

HEBREWS 10:22 NASB

Faith sees the invisible, believes the unbelievable, and receives the impossible.

CORRIE TEN BOOM

Fearing God

Fear God? Aren't we supposed to trust, not fear the Lord? Fear isn't of God, right?

In the following verses we discover the definition of "fearing" God, and it's not what some people might think. The word *fear* is derived from the Greek word *eulabeia*, signifying caution and reverence.

When a godly fear and love are combined, they constitute a heartfelt devotion toward God. To fear the Lord is to reverence, love, respect, and honor Him. There's nothing scary about that!

Therefore, since we receive a kingdom which cannot be shaken, let us show gratitude, by which we may offer to God an acceptable service with reverence and awe; for our God is a consuming fire.

HEBREWS 12:28–29 NASB

Lord, I want my heart to continually be filled with praise and thanksgiving to You. Keep me anchored in the thought that all You do is for my good and glory. Only You are deserving of my praise and adoration. Amen

Saying with a loud voice, Fear God, and give glory to him; for the hour of his judgment is come: and worship him that made heaven, and earth, and the sea, and the fountains of waters.

REVELATION 14:7 KJV

Precious Father, on my own, I am bound to fail. Now that I have put my trust in You, I cannot fail, for You are always the victor, and this knowledge makes me strong where once I was weak. Amen.

"Oh that they had such a heart in them, that they would fear Me and keep all My commandments always, that it may be well with them and with their sons forever!"

DEUTERONOMY 5:29 NASB

Father, I ask for Your wisdom and guidance. Instruct me in the best ways to teach my children about Your great love. I trust You will guide me so I may serve You all the days of my life. Amen.

"Have you no respect for me? Why don't you tremble in my presence? I, the LORD, define the ocean's sandy shoreline as an everlasting boundary that the waters cannot cross. The waves may toss and roar, but they can never pass the boundaries I set."

JEREMIAH 5:22 NLT

Reverence for the Lord is the beginning of wisdom.

ELISABETH ELLIOT

Forgiveness

How do we forgive someone who has wronged us or hurt someone we love? How can we forgive when we don't feel forgiveness?

Corrie ten Boom, survivor of a women's Nazi concentration camp, wrote: "Forgiveness is an act of the will, and the will can function regardless of the temperature of the heart."

For every Christian, forgiveness is a choice. In order to fully receive God's forgiveness we must willingly extend forgiveness to others.

Through an act of her will, Corrie forgave her persecutors and her sister's murderers. Jesus forgave humankind of even more. How can we do less?

Bearing with one another, and forgiving one another,
if anyone has a complaint against another;
even as Christ forgave you, so you also must do.
COLOSSIANS 3:13 NKJV

Lord, give me the strength to forgive others so You will forgive me my own trespasses. Amen.

For if ye forgive men their trespasses, your heavenly Father will also forgive you: But if ye forgive not men their trespasses, neither will your Father forgive your trespasses.

MATTHEW 6:14–15 KJV

Father, show me the way to true forgiveness. I want to do Your will despite my weakness. Be my guide along this difficult path that leads to my own sorely needed forgiveness. Amen.

If My people who are called by My name will humble themselves, and pray and seek My face, and turn from their wicked ways, then I will hear from heaven, and will forgive their sin and heal their land.

2 CHRONICLES 7:14 NKJV

Father, when I am a poor example to someone I meet, grant me forgiveness. Grant those I offend the wisdom to understand that no one is free of sin, but Your grace is sufficient. Amen.

Then Peter came and said to Him, "Lord, how often shall my brother sin against me and I forgive him? Up to seven times?" Jesus said to him, "I do not say to you, up to seven times, but up to seventy times seven."

MATTHEW 18:21–22 NASB

If the wounds of millions are to be healed, what other way is there except through forgiveness?

CATHERINE MARSHALL

Generosity

Each Thanksgiving, Phyllis opens her home to the widows and singles of her church. She spends hours in meal preparations and sets the table with her finest china and best linens. Becky spends eight hours each week babysitting for young moms in need of a break. And for years, Lori and Esther have visited a local nursing home, sharing small gifts and homemade cookies with the residents.

Displays of generosity are as varied and numerous as the human fingerprint. Giving of our time, money, or talents is generous because we are giving of ourselves.

Do not withhold good from those to whom it is due, when it is in your power to act. Do not say to your neighbor, "Come back tomorrow and I'll give it to you"—when you already have it with you.

PROVERBS 3:27–28 NIV

Lord, help me to be as generous. Give me Your guidance. Reveal the needs of my brother and sister—whether they are physical, emotional, or spiritual—and incline my heart to them. Amen.

And He saw also a certain poor widow putting in two mites. So He said, "Truly I say to you that this poor widow has put in more than all; for all these out of their abundance have put in offerings for God, but she out of her poverty put in all the livelihood that she had."

LUKE 21:2–4 NKJV

Lord, show me how to be a godly woman, how to have true contentment that comes from service to You. Help me to reinforce in my home the need to be satisfied with doing Your will. Amen.

"Give, and it will be given to you: good measure, pressed down, shaken together, and running over will be put into your bosom. For with the same measure that you use, it will be measured back to you."

LUKE 6:38 NKJV

Lord, You promise me wonderful rewards when I am charitable. But I cannot answer every request made of me, so I count on You to guide me as to where I should invest my efforts in such a way as to bring You glory. Amen.

Each of you should give what he has decided in your heart to give, not reluctantly or under compulsion, for God loves a cheerful giver.

2 CORINTHIANS 9:7 NIV

It's not how much we give but how much love we put into giving.

MOTHER TERESA

Gentleness

Dr. James Dobson, Christian psychologist and author, recalls the gentleness his wife exhibited whenever she awakened their young daughter from a nap. Standing nearby, Dobson would watch as Shirley gently stirred their child from slumber with her soft, sweet, soothing words. Her genteel manner impacted the renowned psychologist so much that he spoke of it many years later.

How we approach people matters. Are we brazen and critical? Or are we compassionate, seasoning our words with kindness? Gentleness is a fruit of the Spirit that brings much-needed relief in a harsh world.

He tends his flock like a shepherd: He gathers the lambs in his arms and carries them close to his heart; he gently leads those that have young.

ISAIAH 40:11 NIV

Father, You gave me my children to cherish, and that includes being gentle with them. I do treasure them, Lord, so help me to impart Your gentleness to them. Amen.

"Take My yoke upon you and learn from Me, for I am gentle and humble in heart, and YOU WILL FIND REST FOR YOUR SOULS."

MATTHEW 11:29 NASB

Lord, direct me daily to accept and apply the strength that You've offered, so that I will truly have the gentle spirit that You intended me to have. Thank You, Jesus, that I don't have to do this on my own. Amen.

The LORD sustains the humble
but casts the wicked to the ground.
PSALM 147:6 NIV

Father, help me understand faithfulness and to trust in Your love above all else, claiming none of Your glory as a personal reward. Amen.

Now I, Paul, myself am pleading with you by the meekness and gentleness of Christ—who in presence am lowly among you, but being absent am bold toward you.

2 Corinthians 10:1 NKJV

Take my heart and make it your dwelling place so that everyone I touch will be touched also by you!

Alice Joyce Davidson

God's Love

Have you ever read 1 Corinthians 13–the "Love Chapter"? The Living Bible says that love is patient and kind; never boastful, selfish, or rude. Love never demands its own way or is glad about injustice–rather, love rejoices when the truth wins out. Love is loyal no matter the cost. Love always believes the best in us and stands its ground in defending us.

Now substitute the word *love* with "God" and read that paragraph again. You see, God not only loves–He *is* love. No other love in heaven or on earth compares to God's because His very nature defines *agape*–selfless, unconditional–love. And that's how God loves us.

By this the love of God was manifested in us, that God has sent His only begotten Son into the world so that we might live through Him.

1 John 4:9 NASB

Thank You, Jesus, for Your sacrificial love for me. Thank You for the example of true love that You have provided. Amen.

"I will heal their waywardness and love them freely, for my anger has turned away from them."

HOSEA 14:4 NIV

Forgive me, Lord, for those times when I've doubted Your love. Let me close my eyes, hold out my hand, and know that You are there. Thank You for being with me, Father. Amen.

But as it is written: "Eye has not seen, nor ear heard, nor have entered into the heart of man the things which God has prepared for those who love Him."

1 Corinthians 2:9 NKJV

Lord, I know that You are the one at work in me; Your Spirit is a part of me, and You guide my thoughts and actions. Thank You for that. I don't know what I would do if I had to live life on my own. Amen.

And I am convinced that nothing can ever separate us from God's love. Neither death nor life, neither angels nor demons, neither our fears for today nor our worries about tomorrow—not even the powers of hell can separate us from God's love. No power in the sky above or in the earth below—indeed, nothing in all creation will ever be able to separate us from the love of God that is revealed in Christ Jesus our Lord.

ROMANS 8:38–39 NLT

Love has its source in God, for love is the very essence of His being.

KAY ARTHUR

God's Provision

In recent years, a failing economy has caused much distress. People have lost their jobs and homes, and parents wonder how they will support their families. Yet it doesn't take a job loss to experience a financial drain, resulting in a shortage of basic necessities.

The following scriptures encourage us with words of hope and promise. Every Christian has the assurance of God's provision during tough times. As we wisely manage our money and trust in His promises, the Lord supplies—perhaps not our wants—but every one of our needs.

And my God shall supply all your need according to His riches in glory by Christ Jesus.

PHILIPPIANS 4:19 NKJV

Thank You, Father, for giving us all the things we need for life and godliness. You are the Great Provider. Amen.

The lions may grow weak and hungry,
but those who seek the LORD lack no good thing.
PSALM 34:10 NIV

Father, I welcome Your help. You know what I need, and I trust Your provision, knowing You always act in my best interests and want me to have a happy life. Amen.

Once I was young, and now I am old. Yet I have never seen the godly abandoned or their children begging for bread.

PSALM 37:25 NLT

Father, when troubles come, I never have to face them alone. Thank You for always being with me as my refuge and strength. When all else fails, I put my trust in You and am never disappointed. Amen.

Charge them that are rich in this world, that they be not highminded, nor trust in uncertain riches, but in the living God, who giveth us richly all things to enjoy.

1 TIMOTHY 6:17 KJV

Lift up your eyes. Your heavenly Father waits to bless you in inconceivable ways to make your life what you never dreamed it could be.

ANNE ORTLUND

Gratitude

Evangelist Joyce Meyer has said, "Christians need an attitude of gratitude!"

Though we know that God frowns on murmuring and complaining, we do it anyway. We grumble about long stoplights, difficult neighbors, the weather, our jobs, family members, or household chores. Instead of thanking God for our blessings, we approach life with resignation rather than anticipation and gratefulness.

But what if we adjusted our attitude? We might just be happy! God's Word motivates us to discover and maintain a thankful spirit. Try it! Seize an attitude of gratitude.

Blessed be the LORD, that hath given rest unto his people Israel, according to all that he promised: there hath not failed one word of all his good promise, which he promised by the hand of Moses his servant.

1 KINGS 8:56 KJV

Father, thank You for all You have given me, for all You have taught me, and for all the good times still to come. Amen.

O Lord, You have brought up my soul from Sheol;
You have kept me alive, that I would not go down to the pit.

Psalm 30:3 NASB

Father, thanks to You I get to start over, fresh and clean, because You have made me a new person. I now have a lifetime of new days to spend any way I choose. Thank You for Your never-ending forgiveness. Amen.

I will tell of the kindnesses of the LORD, the deeds for which he is to be praised, according to all the LORD has done for us—yes, the many good things he has done for the house of Israel, according to his compassion and many kindnesses.

ISAIAH 63:7 NIV

Thank You for dealing with my sins so thoroughly, Lord—for granting me a new start every day and proclaiming that I am worth saving. Amen.

Whoever regards one day as special does so to the Lord. Whoever eats meat does so to the Lord, for they give thanks to God; and whoever abstains does so to the Lord and gives thanks to God.

ROMANS 14:6 NIV

Simple gratitude helps us experience God at work in every moment of every day.

HARRIET CROSBY

Honesty

The cashier gives you too much money in change. Do you tell her? Out-of-town friends call unexpectedly and ask to stop by. Your house is a mess, you're dead tired, and you're in your pajamas. What do you say?

These scenarios happen all the time, giving us an opportunity to shine with honesty or dim with deceit. God's Word tells us to be aboveboard and upright in our dealings with others.

The old adage says, "Honesty is the best policy." Yet it's more than that. Honesty is a way of life.

Pray for us; for we are confident that we have a good conscience, in all things desiring to live honorably.

HEBREWS 13:18 NKJV

Lord, guide me daily to commit to being truthful. I know I can't expect my family to be honest if I'm not willing to set the example. Help me as I strive to be like You. Amen.

Make it your goal to live a quiet life, minding your own business and working with your hands, just as we instructed you before. Then people who are not Christians will respect the way you live, and you will not need to depend on others.

1 Thessalonians 4:11–12 NLT

Lord, I know I am Your representative here on earth and should give no one the opportunity to reject You because of my actions. When I am within seconds of being a bad example, send me Your peace. Amen.

He who walks righteously and speaks with sincerity, he who rejects unjust gain and shakes his hands so that they hold no bribe; he who stops his ears from hearing about bloodshed and shuts his eyes from looking upon evil; he will dwell on the heights, his refuge will be the impregnable rock; his bread will be given him, his water will be sure.

ISAIAH 33:15–16 NASB

I am Your ambassador, Lord, and every day I try to show Your love to those who do not know You. I pray that when the time comes, You will find me worthy. Amen.

"I will maintain my righteousness and never let go of it; my conscience will not reproach me as long as I live."
JOB 27:6 NIV

Do not do what you would undo if caught.
LEAH ARENDT

Honor

To honor is to highly esteem someone for their integrity, honesty, uprightness, or courage. We pay homage to our veterans for their service to our country; we laud athletes, students, entertainers, ministers, and others who achieve excellence in their fields. In other words, we honor people we value and deem worthy of our respect.

The following verses tell us to honor the Lord with our tithes, our adoration, and everything we have. Far above all others, God is worthy of *all* our honor and praise.

Honor the Lord with your possessions,
and with the firstfruits of all your increase.
Proverbs 3:9 NKJV

Father, praising You and rejoicing in You must be high on my priority list. Proclaiming Your love to others must never be lacking in my life. Thank You that I am able to rejoice in You! Amen.

Fix these words of mine in your hearts and minds; tie them as symbols on your hands and bind them on your foreheads. Teach them to your children, talking about them when you sit at home and when you walk along the road, when you lie down and when you get up.

Deuteronomy 11:18–19 NIV

Father, help me teach my children the way to honor You in all we do. Let me be as kind and patient with my children as You are with me. Amen.

Children, obey your parents because you belong to the Lord, for this is the right thing to do. "Honor your father and mother." This is the first commandment with a promise: If you honor your father and mother, "things will go well for you, and you will have a long life on the earth."

Ephesians 6:1–3 NLT

Father, raising obedient, loving children requires me to show gentleness and patience, not threats or harshness. I pray that You will teach me how to soften each correction with the same love I receive from You. Amen.

She is more precious than jewels; and nothing you desire compares with her. Long life is in her right hand; in her left hand are riches and honor.

PROVERBS 3:15–16 NASB

Let our actions make us worthy of the blessing we have received and [pray] that God will continue to bless us!

DIANE ALBERS

Hope

Have you ever hoped for something? Maybe a bigger house? A smaller dress size? A day to yourself? Or maybe more serious things like a physical healing or restoration of your marriage?

The word *hope* in the Greek translation is *elpis*, meaning "confident expectation in the unseen future" or "the happy expectation of good."

Hope launches a positive outlook. Without it, lives remain fragmented and broken, personal dreams go unrealized, and sick hearts lose the capacity to cope. Hope tells you to hold on in anticipation and expectation—because something good is just ahead!

For I know the thoughts that I think toward you, says the LORD, thoughts of peace and not of evil, to give you a future and a hope.

JEREMIAH 29:11 NKJV

Father God, the joy has gone out of my life. I need Your reassurance that You will never give me a burden without helping me bear it. Be my strong hope of a better future. Amen.

"Blessed is the man who trusts in the LORD,
and whose hope is the LORD."

JEREMIAH 17:7 NKJV

Lord, You are my hope in an often hopeless world. You are my hope of heaven, my hope of peace, my hope of change, purpose, and unconditional love. Fill the reservoir of my heart to overflowing with the joy that real hope brings. Amen.

I pray that God, the source of hope, will fill you completely with joy and peace because you trust in him. Then you will overflow with confident hope through the power of the Holy Spirit.

ROMANS 15:13 NLT

When all hope seems lost, Lord, be with those who suffer. Help them to never abandon hope, for all things are possible with You. Amen.

And we desire that each one of you show the same diligence to the full assurance of hope until the end.

HEBREWS 6:11 NKJV

Optimism is the faith that leads to achievement. Nothing can be done without hope and confidence.

HELEN KELLER

Hospitality

Women and hospitality go together like coffee and cream. Generally, women are the ones who host family gatherings, church dinners, kids' birthday parties, and so much more.

Back in the 1930s and '40s, vagabonds would often go house-to-house for food. Without hesitation, the woman of the house would serve the stranger a hot meal. Of course, that kind of hospitality is dangerous today. Yet we should continue to open our homes and give to those we *do* know.

Do not forget to entertain strangers, for by so doing some have unwittingly entertained angels.

HEBREWS 13:2 NKJV

Lord, I want my house to be Your house–a house of prayer, a place of comfort and peace, a refuge to those in need. Help me make our home a blessing for all who pass through its door. Amen.

Use hospitality one to another without grudging.

1 PETER 4:9 KJV

Father God, it seems my cynical attitude is keeping me from performing acts of hospitality. Please give me the faith and strength to do what needs to be done, not because I want a reward but because it is an honor to do Your work. Amen.

Wisdom has built her house; she has set up its seven pillars. She has prepared her meat and mixed her wine; she has also set her table. She has sent out her servants, and she calls from the highest point of the city, "Let all who are simple come to my house!" To those who have no sense she says, "Come, eat my food and drink the wine I have mixed."

PROVERBS 9:1–5 NIV

Father, be with us today and stay near as we strive to raise our family in a way that will please You and allow us to accomplish whatever You have planned. Use our home as a place to glorify You and reach out to others. Amen.

"Instead, invite the poor, the crippled, the lame, and the blind. Then at the resurrection of the righteous, God will reward you for inviting those who could not repay you."

LUKE 14:13–14 NLT

Just allow your guest to feel at ease because you are, whatever the state of your house. This is an important element to being a gracious host.

LINDA DAVIS ZUMBEHL

Humility

Nineteenth-century missionary Mary Slessor said: "Blessed is the man or woman who is able to serve cheerfully in the second rank—a big test."

Serving in the limelight is one thing, but serving absent of accolades and applause is another. Those who take a backseat and work as hard as if they were in the front seat are diligent. But those who take a backseat and have no thought of taking credit for their deeds are humble.

Jesus said, "The first shall be last and the last shall be first" in God's kingdom. Humility leads to greatness, and great people are the ones who are humble.

Be of the same mind toward one another;
do not be haughty in mind, but associate with the lowly.
Do not be wise in your own estimation.

ROMANS 12:16 NASB

Father, I need a reminder that what I should be is a servant. I get so wrapped up in the need to maintain order that I forget my job–to meet the needs of others. Please give me a servant's heart. Amen.

But made Himself of no reputation, taking the form of a bondservant, and coming in the likeness of men. And being found in appearance as a man, He humbled Himself and became obedient to the point of death, even the death of the cross. Therefore God also has highly exalted Him and given Him the name which is above every name.

PHILIPPIANS 2:7–9 NKJV

Lord, thank You for asking Jesus to pay the high price for what I've done. The thought of His sacrifice and Your unending grace humbles me beyond words. "Thank You" will never be enough. Amen.

In the same way, you who are younger, submit yourselves to your elders. All of you, clothe yourselves with humility toward one another, because, "God opposes the proud but shows favor to the humble." Humble yourselves, therefore, under God's mighty hand, that he may lift you up in due time.

1 PETER 5:5–6 NIV

Vows to You must be kept, Father. You not only remember Your promises to us, You never forget our promises to You. Help me treat my vows to You seriously, Lord. If sacrifices are required of me, let me bear them in faith. Amen.

Humble yourselves in the presence of the Lord, and He will exalt you.

JAMES 4:10 NASB

All of the charm and beauty a woman may have amounts to nothing if her ambitions are self-centered. But if she reflects her Creator and assumes the posture of a graceful servant, she cannot help but command high respect and love.

JEANNE HENDRICKS

Joy

Do you know someone who has a spirit of joy? No matter what happens in life, she always has an uplifting word and a glowing smile. She sparkles with joy brighter than polished diamonds and, not surprisingly, everyone enjoys her company.

The scriptures encourage us to delight in the Lord that way—to illuminate with joy about our salvation and the goodness of God. Our joy should shine in such a way that it lights the pathway to lead others to Christ.

One day, we will rejoice in heaven. That fact alone should cause us to jump for joy!

Be glad in the Lord and rejoice, you righteous;
and shout for joy, all you upright in heart!

Psalm 32:11 NKJV

There's no mistaking, Lord. You've made it clear that I'm to be joyful in each and every task. The next time I'm tempted to complain about the mounds of work, remind me to turn the murmuring into praise. Amen.

Shout joyfully to the LORD, all the earth. Serve the LORD with gladness; come before Him with joyful singing.

PSALM 100:1–2 NASB

I am not worthy of Your gifts of mercy and forgiveness, Father, but I accept them with joy. Amen.

"The master was full of praise. 'Well done, my good and faithful servant. You have been faithful in handling this small amount, so now I will give you many more responsibilities. Let's celebrate together!'"

MATTHEW 25:21 NLT

Father, fill our hearts full of You and Your Word; then we can sing with grace and joy. My family and I can proclaim Your goodness to all those we meet. What a blessing! Amen.

Singing psalms and hymns and spiritual songs among yourselves, and making music to the Lord in your hearts.

EPHESIANS 5:19 NLT

Laughter lightens the load.

PATSY CLAIRMONT

Kindness

Years ago, Oprah Winfrey encouraged her audience to engage in "random acts of kindness." She led the crusade through personal example with deeds such as paying the toll for the person in the vehicle behind her. Her message was simple: Extend one act of kindness to a stranger each day.

Kindness is rooted in a giving heart. The virtue is displayed in small ways like driving an elderly patient to the doctor, cooking a meal for a shut-in, babysitting for a busy mom, or simply sharing a smile.

When kindness is the rule, there's nothing random about it.

Since God chose you to be the holy people he loves,
you must clothe yourselves with tenderhearted mercy,
kindness, humility, gentleness, and patience.

COLOSSIANS 3:12 NLT

Lord, You welcomed me into Your family with love and acceptance. Help me be as kind to others as You have been to me–cheerfully welcoming everyone. Amen.

And to godliness brotherly kindness; and to brotherly kindness charity. For if these things be in you, and abound. . .ye shall neither be barren nor unfruitful in the knowledge of our Lord Jesus Christ.

2 Peter 1:7–8 KJV

Lord, may I never hesitate to forgive anyone when You have already forgiven me. Amen.

He can have compassion on those who are ignorant and going astray, since he himself is also subject to weakness.

HEBREWS 5:2 NKJV

True love is kind, not prideful or self-seeking. Lord, fill me with compassion for my fellow Christians so I might be a godly example of love and understanding. I want to emulate You, Jesus. Amen.

"Give to the one who asks you, and do not turn away from the one who wants to borrow from you."
MATTHEW 5:42 NIV

Let no one ever come to you without leaving better and happier. Be the living expression of God's kindness: kindness in your face, kindness in your eyes, kindness in your smile.
MOTHER TERESA

Love of God

Do you love God? Some would think that a trick question. Of course every Christian loves God! Don't they?

The following scriptures address this subject. They tell us that if we love God we will—among other things—seek Him and keep His commandments. Placing God first and desiring His will above our own demonstrates our love and devotion to the One who has done, and continues to do, so much for us.

Loving God is more than lip service, it's God-service.

The Lord watches over all who love him,
but all the wicked he will destroy.
Psalm 145:20 NIV

Lord, I really want to grow spiritually. I need to—for my own daily walk with You and, most importantly, because You've commanded me to. Thank You for giving me the strength to fulfill your commands and to grow spiritually. Amen.

That Christ may dwell in your hearts through faith; that you, being rooted and grounded in love, may be able to comprehend with all the saints what is the width and length and depth and height—to know the love of Christ which passes knowledge; that you may be filled with all the fullness of God.

EPHESIANS 3:17–19 NKJV

Lord, I pray that my children and their children and each successive generation will understand that all the glory for our many blessings belongs to You. Without You we would be nothing and would have nothing. Amen.

And we know that all things work together for good to them that love God, to them who are the called according to his purpose.

ROMANS 8:28 KJV

Thank You for the work You have given me, Father, with its opportunities to be of service to others and to You. You have made me a woman of value, and my contribution is great. Amen.

"He who has My commandments and keeps them is the one who loves Me; and he who loves Me will be loved by My Father, and I will love him and will disclose Myself to him."
JOHN 14:21 NASB

The greatest need in the world today is love. . . . More love for each other and more love for God above!
HELEN STEINER RICE

Love for Others

God commands us to love others, and guess what? That includes our enemies, too. It's easy to love those who love us or—at the very least—to love those who are somewhat lovable. But our enemies?

Enemy is a strong word, but you get the picture. It describes anyone who is hostile or adversarial toward you. Like the coworker who diminishes your job position while aggrandizing hers. Or the neighbor who persistently gossips about you despite your efforts to help her.

God's love compels us to love, forgive, understand, and pray for one another. . .even the unlovable.

Be devoted to one another in brotherly love.
Honor one another above yourselves.
ROMANS 12:10 NIV

Lord, help me not to be quick to judge or oppose love between others. Let me give love time to do its work. I may never see the result I want, but I am sure it is in Your hands. Amen.

Thou shalt not avenge, nor bear any grudge against the children of thy people, but thou shalt love thy neighbour as thyself: I am the Lord.

Leviticus 19:18 KJV

Lord, thank You for Your attention to those who struggle, for Your provision, and for the promise that their dreams will eventually come true. I wish them the contentment I am now enjoying. Amen.

Dear friends, let us love one another, for love comes from God. Everyone who loves has been born of God and knows God. Whoever does not love does not know God, because God is love. This is how God showed his love among us: He sent his one and only Son into the world that we might live through him. This is love: not that we loved God, but that he loved us and sent his Son as an atoning sacrifice for our sins. Dear friends, since God so loved us, we also ought to love one another.

1 John 4:7–11 NIV

Lord, help me to show compassion for my children and also for strangers. You were the best example. You loved everyone, Lord. Help me do the same, and in doing so set an example for my children. Amen.

Finally, all of you be of one mind, having compassion for one another; love as brothers, be tenderhearted, be courteous.

1 Peter 3:8 NKJV

If I put my own good name before the other's highest good, then I know nothing of Calvary love.

Amy Carmichael

Meekness

How can a Type-A lady, with an exuberant, take-charge, outgoing personality, exhibit meekness? Wouldn't that contradict who she really is?

Jesus not only encourages meekness in His beatitudes, He described Himself as "meek and lowly in heart" (Matthew 11:29 KJV). Yet Jesus was no pushover.

Meekness isn't our outward behavior, but an inwrought grace of the soul. It is a tempered spirit fully surrendered to God, one that accepts His dealings without dispute or resistance. Meekness demonstrates full devotion to and humility before God.

Jesus said that the meek will inherit the earth. And that includes Type-A personalities, too.

Brethren, if a man is overtaken in any trespass, you who are spiritual restore such a one in a spirit of gentleness, considering yourself lest you also be tempted. Bear one another's burdens, and so fulfill the law of Christ.

GALATIANS 6:1–2 NKJV

Lord, I want to help bring others to You, to be judged a virtuous woman for Your sake, not for any glory that might come to me. Use me as You see fit, because any work You give me is an honor. Amen.

Seek the Lord, all you meek of the earth, who have upheld His justice. Seek righteousness, seek humility. It may be that you will be hidden in the day of the Lord's anger.

ZEPHANIAH 2:3 NKJV

Thank You for the times I am humbled, Lord. You are always here—to listen, to forgive, and to heal. Lord, help me to be repentant, to be willing to be brought low. Heal me, Lord. Amen.

Take my yoke upon you, and learn of me; for I am meek and lowly in heart: and ye shall find rest unto your souls.

MATTHEW 11:29 KJV

I want my life to be a sacrifice for You, Lord. Help me live a life of praise for You before my children. Guide me in showing my children how to make the sacrifice of praise to You. Amen.

"Blessed are the gentle, for they shall inherit the earth."
MATTHEW 5:5 NASB

We can do no great things; only small things with great love.
MOTHER TERESA

Mercy

God is merciful. If He wasn't, most of us would be in big trouble!

The Greek translation of mercy means "an outward manifestation of pity; it assumes need on the part of him who receives it, and the resources adequate to meet the need on the part of him who shows it."

If we love when wronged, we show mercy. If we give or forgive despite our grievances, we exhibit mercy. And if we understand those who are misunderstood, we are merciful.

Teamed with goodness, mercy shall follow believers all the days of their lives (Psalm 23:6). Lord, have mercy!

Be ye therefore merciful, as your Father also is merciful.

LUKE 6:36 KJV

Father, help me remember that my priorities are not necessarily the priorities of those I love, so please give me the sense to step back and allow everyone a little leeway to lead their own lives. Help me be supportive, not bossy. Amen.

He has told you, O man, what is good; and what does the LORD require of you but to do justice, to love kindness, and to walk humbly with your God?

MICAH 6:8 NASB

Lord, may those I work with always see You in my life and be brought closer to You though me. Amen.

"He saved us, not because of the righteous things we had done, but because of his mercy. He washed away our sins, giving us a new birth and new life through the Holy Spirit. He generously poured out the Spirit upon us through Jesus Christ our Savior. Because of his grace he declared us righteous and gave us confidence that we will inherit eternal life."

TITUS 3:5–7 NLT

Lord, I don't know if I'll ever understand why You sacrificed Yourself for me. But, from the depths of my being, I want to shout praises to You and also tell the whole world what You did for all of us. Amen.

Let the wicked forsake his way, and the unrighteous man his thoughts: and let him return unto the LORD, and he will have mercy upon him; and to our God, for he will abundantly pardon.

ISAIAH 55:7 KJV

God deals with us from a merciful posture; His arms are open, His words are healing, He wants sinners to return to Him.

MARTIE STOWELL

Obedience

Elisabeth Elliot, wife of martyred missionary Jim Elliot, said: "God is God. Because He is God, He is worthy of my trust and obedience."

A successful Christian walk is based on our obedience to Christ. In fact, to obey God is to love, serve, trust, and believe Him.

Consider how it pleases you when your child obeys you without question or resistance. He or she simply trusts you at your word and does what you ask. Nice, huh? The same is true of our heavenly Father. It pleases Him when we trust Him enough to obey.

"Now then, if you will indeed obey My voice and keep My covenant, then you shall be My own possession among all the peoples, for all the earth is Mine."
EXODUS 19:5 NASB

When Your purpose is revealed to me, Father, help me to accept my responsibility and do Your will. Amen.

"You shall therefore keep His statutes and His commandments which I command you today, that it may go well with you and with your children after you, and that you may prolong your days in the land which the LORD your God is giving you for all time."

DEUTERONOMY 4:40 NKJV

Father, I admit that once in a while I have a temper tantrum, disputing Your guidance and wanting my own way, but You have never been wrong. Thank You for Your love and patience, for I will always need Your guidance. Amen.

So if you ignore the least commandment and teach others to do the same, you will be called the least in the Kingdom of Heaven. But anyone who obeys God's laws and teaches them will be called great in the Kingdom of Heaven.

MATTHEW 5:19 NLT

Lord, I want to obey You in everything and also lead my family to obey You. Through our obedience to You, help us to reach many people for Your kingdom. Amen.

"If you are willing and obedient,
you will eat the best from the land."
ISAIAH 1:19 NIV

The only way I will keep a pliable, obedient spirit in the larger decisions is to look to Him and to obey in the smaller ones.
CATHERINE MARSHALL

Patience

Patience is a lost virtue in today's fast-paced, I-want-it-now society. We want results and we want them immediately! Just ask any woman on a diet. After a week or so, some of us fall off the wagon when the number on the scale doesn't drop quickly enough.

Our impatience surfaces in other ways, too—everything from waiting in a store checkout line to waiting for answered prayer.

Attaining patience is a process, often birthed from endurance on the battlefield of trials. Yet patience is a virtue worth working—and waiting—for.

And a servant of the Lord must not quarrel but be gentle to all, able to teach, patient.

2 TIMOTHY 2:24 NKJV

Put a new song in my mouth, Lord. Let others see me being patient and waiting on You, no matter what difficulty I'm facing. Help them learn the same song of joy that You are giving me. Amen.

Be still in the presence of the LORD, and wait patiently for him to act. Don't worry about evil people who prosper or fret about their wicked schemes. Stop being angry! Turn from your rage! Do not lose your temper—it only leads to harm. For the wicked will be destroyed, but those who trust in the LORD will possess the land.

PSALM 37:7–9 NLT

Lord, I want to learn to be patient and trust in You. I know that You will hear my cries and I will be blessed. Thank You for this blessing. Amen.

Therefore be patient, brethren, until the coming of the Lord. The farmer waits for the precious produce of the soil, being patient about it, until it gets the early and late rains. You too be patient; strengthen your hearts, for the coming of the Lord is near.

JAMES 5:7–8 NASB

Renew me. Give me the ability I need to be patient, no matter what trouble is around me. Let my joyful hope and faithful prayers build up my patience. Amen.

And so, having patiently waited, he obtained the promise.

HEBREWS 6:15 NASB

Obedience is the
fruit of faith; patience,
the bloom on the fruit.

CHRISTINA ROSSETTI

Peace

How do you describe peace? A day spent at the beach? An afternoon without phone calls and to-do lists? How about a stress-free week? Those things may initiate peace, but they are rarely the source of it.

God gives us a peace that surpasses human understanding—the kind of peace that prevails in the most difficult situations or alarming circumstances. Only the Lord can administer tranquility in the midst of life's storms.

Need peace? Relax and bask in the peace that only God provides.

I pray that God, the source of hope, will fill you completely with joy and peace because you trust in him. Then you will overflow with confident hope through the power of the Holy Spirit.

ROMANS 15:13 NLT

Lord, help untangle my emotions and sort my jumbled thoughts. Calm my restless spirit. Help me experience Your supernatural peace in a real and tangible way. Amen.

For, "the one who desires life, to love and see good days,
must keep his tongue from evil and his lips from speaking deceit.
He must turn away from evil and do good;
he must seek peace and pursue it."

1 Peter 3:10–11 NASB

Heavenly Father, I long for Your peace in my heart. Please take every anxious thread, every tightly pulled knot of uncertainty, sorrow, conflict, and disappointment into Your gentle, loving hands. Amen.

And He will judge between the nations, and will render decisions for many peoples; and they will hammer their swords into plowshares and their spears into pruning hooks. Nation will not lift up sword against nation, and never again will they learn war.

Isaiah 2:4 NASB

Lord, no matter what happens to upset us on the surface, You are in our innermost being, bringing peace and comfort. Thank You that we can always trust You. Amen.

"I am leaving you with a gift—peace of mind and heart. And the peace I give is a gift the world cannot give. So don't be troubled or afraid."

JOHN 14:27 NLT

When the presence of the Lord really becomes your experience, you will actually discover that you have gradually begun to love this silence and peaceful rest which come with His presence.

MADAME GUYON

Perseverance

You've tried everything to no avail. Now what? You've prayed for a loved one for years, but nothing changes. What do you do?

The Lord tells us that after we've done everything we know to do, and have said everything we know to say, to stand. In other words, persevere. Keep believing, praying, and standing in faith.

The same holds true for every area of our lives. We must hold steady in the face of adversity, doubt, or apparent failure. Why? Because God is faithful if we will only stand fast and persevere against all odds.

"To him who overcomes I will grant to sit with Me on My throne, as I also overcame and sat down with My Father on His throne."

REVELATION 3:21 NKJV

Thank You for Your promise to preserve me if I love You, Father. I know that this is an eternal promise. What more incentive do I need to pursue a right walk with You? Keep me on the right path, Lord. Amen.

Though he fall, he shall not be utterly cast down;
for the LORD upholds him with His hand.

PSALM 37:24 NKJV

This burden is heavy, Lord. There are days when I don't know how much longer I can go on. But Your Word says that You will provide a way of escape. You help us carry our burdens. Thank You for Your promise. Amen.

Therefore take up the whole armor of God, that you may be able to withstand in the evil day, and having done all, to stand.

EPHESIANS 6:13 NKJV

Thank You, Lord, for being so faithful. Thank You for Your compassion—that is just the right amount to get me through the day. Amen.

These trials will show that your faith is genuine. It is being tested as fire tests and purifies gold—though your faith is far more precious than mere gold. So when your faith remains strong through many trials, it will bring you much praise and glory and honor on the day when Jesus Christ is revealed to the whole world.

1 Peter 1:7 NLT

You may have to fight a battle more than once to win it.

Margaret Thatcher

Power

Workshops, conferences, books, and magazines all herald the attributes of empowerment and what it can mean in a woman's life. We long to fortify ourselves with the knowledge, wisdom, capabilities, and tools that will give us the power to become or do something greater than ourselves.

The scriptures talk a lot about power, too—the power of God. As the Lord empowers us through the Holy Spirit, we change in ways we never dreamed and accomplish the seemingly impossible with His help. The truth is, self-empowerment often fades into futility, but God's power empowers the powerless continually.

For the Kingdom of God is not just a lot of talk; it is living by God's power.

1 CORINTHIANS 4:20 NLT

Heavenly Father, my greatest responsibility as Your child is to share Your power with others. My family, my neighbors, my coworkers—so many people need to hear Your Word. Make me attentive to each opportunity You present to me. Amen.

Now to Him who is able to do exceedingly abundantly above all that we ask or think, according to the power that works in us.

EPHESIANS 3:20 NKJV

Given unto You Lord, You told me to give and that if I do, it shall be given to me. You don't say what "it" is, but Your generosity is unmatched and Your blessings are always wonderful. Thank You! Amen.

Seek the LORD and His strength; seek His face continually.

1 CHRONICLES 16:11 NASB

Father, it often seems that might makes right and I stand no chance, but I know Your power can overcome whatever evil men might plan. When I am in despair, fill me with faith in Your justice. Amen.

"The LORD your God is with you, the Mighty Warrior who saves. He will take great delight in you; in his love he will no longer rebuke you but, will rejoice over you with singing."

ZEPHANIAH 3:17 NIV

The stone still stood there in that quiet garden, a reminder of the reality of the problem we all must live with; but Christ had moved it to one side so very easily, demonstrating His resurrection power on our behalf.

JILL BRISCOE

Prayer

A mother prays for her child at the foot of a tear-stained bed. An elderly woman sits in a wheelchair interceding for her church. A grandmother kneels at the kitchen sink to pray for her grandchildren. A young woman sits in a classroom, whispering a prayer for a friend, and a little girl places her hand on her sick puppy and prays.

Prayer is simply talking to God. Lofty words and pious phrases are unnecessary—only a pure, honest, and sincere heart matters. God's power is unleashed through prayer. So pray often, anywhere, anytime.

"At that time you won't need to ask me for anything. I tell you the truth, you will ask the Father directly, and he will grant your request because you use my name. You haven't done this before. Ask, using my name, and you will receive, and you will have abundant joy."

JOHN 16:23-24 NLT

I understand the need to pray, I am just not the best at remembering to pray. I know prayer works and changes things! I need to be more consistent and intentional about praying. Lord - please help me to put prayer higher on my priority list!

Lord, when I see how You have interceded on my behalf, I want to fall on my face before You. My prayers have been answered in miraculous ways. In times when all I could see was darkness, you provided light and power and hope. Amen.

"If you then, being evil, know how to give good gifts to your children, how much more will your Father who is in heaven give good things to those who ask Him!"

MATTHEW 7:11 NKJV

Lord, I'm grateful that I can show my children where to turn in times of trouble. They don't have to try to do it all themselves, because we are all Your children. Amen.

Rejoice in our confident hope.
Be patient in trouble, and keep on praying.

ROMANS 12:12 NLT

Father, I get discouraged when I don't know which way to go. Remind me that You are right behind me, telling me which way to turn. Help me to be quiet and listen for Your guidance. Amen.

"If my people, who are called by my name, will humble themselves and pray and seek my face and turn from their wicked ways, then will I hear from heaven and will forgive their sin and will heal their land."

2 CHRONICLES 7:14 NIV

Prayer is an indispensable part of our relationship with Jesus Christ.

LAUREL OKE LOGAN

Pride

Have you noticed that boasting has become an admirable attribute? (To clarify: Confidence in one's abilities or talents is different from bragging about them.) With much bravado, women from the boardroom to the catwalk herald their gifts and talents with more intensity than an on-the-scene journalist broadcasting breaking news.

Pride is not only admissible in the world, it's expected. To God, however, pride is sin. A proud and haughty spirit is unattractive and unacceptable to the King of kings. Besides, any king's daughter would rather brag about her heavenly Father's attributes than about her own.

"Talk no more so very proudly; let no arrogance come from your mouth, for the LORD is the God of knowledge; and by Him actions are weighed."

1 SAMUEL 2:3 NKJV

Father, please don't let me fall into the trap of false pride. Whatever small beauty I bring into this world is only a tiny reflection of Your beauty, Your creation, Your perfection. Amen.

Live in harmony with one another. Do not be proud, but be willing to associate with people of low position. Do not be conceited.

ROMANS 12:16 NIV

Lord, I'm called to live a godly life—not by childishness but by Your grace and virtue. Thank You for Your provision. Amen.

For by the grace given me I say to every one of you:
Do not think of yourself more highly than you ought, but rather think of yourself with sober judgment, in accordance with the measure of faith God has distributed to each of you.

ROMANS 12:3 NIV

Lord, I need an attitude adjustment that can only come from You. Let me be a cheerful worker. Resolve my conflicted feelings and give me Your peace. Amen.

Pride goes before destruction, and a haughty spirit before stumbling.
PROVERBS 16:18 NASB

Why are we not far more frightened of what pride can do? Pride can cost us—and probably those after us.
BETH MOORE

Protection

As women, we walk with caution to our car or on the street at night. We warn our daughters to guard themselves against possible intruders or attacks. Mothers use child-safety products to protect toddlers from harm, and we teach our children to avoid strangers and to look both ways before crossing the street.

Similarly, God protects us. He provides a refuge in life's storms with the assurance that He is with us in every situation. He takes extra precaution to guide, assist, instruct, and protect us each day. He is our help, our shield, and our best protection.

For You are my rock and my fortress; therefore,
for Your name's sake, lead me and guide me.

PSALM 31:3 NKJV

Lord, I thank You for Your guidance and protection day after day. Although I never know what the day will bring, You have a plan and I trust in You. Amen.

But whoever listens to me will dwell safely,
and will be secure, without fear of evil.
PROVERBS 1:33 NKJV

There are times, Lord, when I feel as if You've forgotten me. How could I let those feelings of being forsaken overwhelm me? Help me to remember that the Creator of the entire universe holds me in His hands! Amen.

The LORD is my rock, my fortress and my deliverer;
my God is my rock, in whom I take refuge, my shield
and the horn of my salvation, my stronghold.

PSALM 18:2 NIV

Lord, Your promise of protection gives me a secure feeling. I'm surrounded by Your love and protection. Because You love me and care for me, I can do the same for my children. Thank You for the peace this brings. Amen.

God is our refuge and strength, always ready to help in times of trouble. So we will not fear when earthquakes come and the mountains crumble into the sea. Let the oceans roar and foam. Let the mountains tremble as the waters surge!

PSALM 46:1–3 NLT

God will never lead you where His strength cannot keep you.

BARBARA JOHNSON

Rest

Most women are doers, proficient in multitasking. We cook dinner as we do laundry and assist our kids with homework. We schedule appointments via cell phone while we grocery shop. We answer e-mails while paying bills. And the moment we stop, our minds spin as we relive the day.

Although rest is essential to our spiritual, physical, and emotional health, it often gets lost like a stray sock in the dryer. God wants His people to rest, and this section of scriptures emphasizes the benefits of and need for a break.

So take a breather. Rest.

I will both lay me down in peace, and sleep:
for thou, LORD, only makest me dwell in safety.

PSALM 4:8 KJV

Heavenly Father, I find it hard to find time to relax. Thank You for making me to lie down even when I don't want to. Thank You for leading me beside quiet waters when I need the solace. Amen.

Rest in the LORD, and wait patiently for him:
fret not thyself because of him who prospereth in his way,
because of the man who bringeth wicked devices to pass.
PSALM 37:7 KJV

Father, give me Your peace and an understanding that all things work together for good when I follow Your will. Amen.

Those who live in the shelter of the Most High
will find rest in the shadow of the Almighty.
PSALM 91:1 NLT

Father, as long as I trust in Your presence, I have nothing to worry about. Nothing can separate me from You, because You are the strong protector, the mighty One who watches over me always. I praise You, Lord, and rest in Your arms. Amen.

"And you would be secure, because there is hope; yes, you would dig around you, and take your rest in safety."
JOB 11:18 NKJV

Again and again, I've found Him faithful to respond, and the closer I move to Him, the safer I feel and the better I rest.
PATSY CLAIRMONT

Righteousness

What is righteousness? What can we do to attain it? Is right living the ticket? Or is there something more we should know or do?

The definition of *righteousness* includes the following: "A quality or character of uprightness; an attribute of God and whatever or whoever conforms to the revealed will of God."

Contrary to what some believe, God's righteousness is only attainable through faith in Christ, not through obedience to a prescribed set of laws or good deeds (Ephesians 2:8–9).

Do you desire righteousness? Accept Christ and follow His Word.

Do you not know that the unrighteous will not inherit the kingdom of God?

If we confess our sins, he is faithful and just and will forgive us our sins and purify us from all unrighteousness.

1 John 1:9 NIV

Father, on my worst days I feel totally unworthy. But I know You have promised to cleanse me from all unrighteousness, to wipe away my guilt and make me whole if I confess my sins. Amen.

"If you fully obey the Lord your God and carefully keep all his commands that I am giving you today, the Lord your God will set you high above all the nations of the world."
Deuteronomy 28:1 NLT

Lord, You stand before the throne of Your Father and claim me as Your own, exempt from sin and judgment. Because of Your sacrifice, I am made worthy. Thank You. Amen.

The LORD hears his people when they call to him for help.
He rescues them from all their troubles.

PSALM 34:17 NLT

Lord, You are made strong in my weaknesses. I need Your help to remember that I should count it all joy when I am faced with trials and suffering. Amen.

For He made Him who knew no sin to be sin for us,
that we might become the righteousness of God in Him.
2 Corinthians 5:21 NKJV

We do not have to be qualified to be holy.
Madeleine L'Engle

Scripture

Is the Bible just an ancient history book? What significance do the scriptures have in modern society? As the following verses indicate, the scriptures are the life-giving, soul-sustaining, power-packed, anointed words of God! They provide us with the spiritual nutrients necessary for daily living.

God's Word reveals God's will and character to us, bringing salvation, healing, deliverance, hope, peace, wisdom, guidance, and restoration to those who read its pages.

Just an ancient history book inapplicable to today's lifestyle and issues? Read on.

Your word is a lamp to my feet and a light to my path.
PSALM 119:105 NASB

Lord, guide me so that all I am and do will point the way for others, that they also can enjoy the benefits of salvation and join their voices in praise of Your Father in heaven. Amen.

And that from a child thou hast known the holy scriptures, which are able to make thee wise unto salvation through faith which is in Christ Jesus.

2 TIMOTHY 3:15 KJV

Father, I know it is Your will for me to understand Your Word, and You've given me the Holy Spirit to guide me. Help me to take advantage of this great blessing. Amen.

Let the word of Christ dwell in you richly in all wisdom, teaching and admonishing one another in psalms and hymns and spiritual songs, singing with grace in your hearts to the Lord.

COLOSSIANS 3:16 NKJV

Lord, as I read and study Your Word and hear sermons preached about it, I still have questions and much to learn. I ask that You give me a clear understanding of what You are saying to me through it. Amen.

For the word of God is living and powerful, and sharper than any two-edged sword, piercing even to the division of soul and spirit, and of joints and marrow, and is a discerner of the thoughts and intents of the heart.

HEBREWS 4:12 NKJV

How much of a calm and gentle spirit you achieve, then, will depend on how regularly and consistently, persistently and obediently you partake of the Word of God, your spiritual food.

SHIRLEY RICE

Seeking God

I once lost my young son in an interactive playroom at Disney World. Panic set in as I scoured every area. About to notify security, I raced to the escalator where Jeff stood sobbing. "Where were you?" he whimpered, as if I was the one who was lost.

Similarly, God isn't lost–we are. Our search for Him begins when we realize that. Most of us seek God when we're afraid, discouraged, sick, or sad. But God desires for us to seek Him because we yearn to know Him. These passages reveal how God blesses and rewards those who diligently seek Him.

Sow with a view to righteousness, reap in accordance with kindness; break up your fallow ground, for it is time to seek the LORD until He comes to rain righteousness on you.

HOSEA 10:12 NASB

Father, my daily problems come and go; yet if I remain steadfast and dedicated, doing the work You have given me to do, I am confident that my reward awaits me. Thank You, Lord. Amen.

At night my soul longs for You, indeed, my spirit within me seeks You diligently; for when the earth experiences Your judgments the inhabitants of the world learn righteousness.

Isaiah 26:9 NASB

Lord, there are many times when I need You and Your Word to guide me. Lead me and help me become an overcomer. Amen.

Therefore if you have been raised up with Christ, keep seeking the things above, where Christ is, seated at the right hand of God.

COLOSSIANS 3:1 NASB

Help me invest my time in more worthy pursuits, Lord, ones that will provide lasting satisfaction. I'm not sure what You will ask of me, but I am willing to try anything You recommend and give any resulting praise to You. Amen.

"Then if my people who are called by my name will humble themselves and pray and seek my face and turn from their wicked ways, I will hear from heaven and will forgive their sins and restore their land."

2 CHRONICLES 7:14 NLT

For it is impossible to be in the presence of Jesus and not be changed.

JOANNA WEAVER

Self-Control

Pastries line the table. "Have one," the hostess says. "Thanks, but I'm dieting," you respond. "One won't hurt," she prods, handing you a chocolate tart. Soon one tart turns into three with a side dish of strawberry cheesecake. "I'll resume my diet tomorrow," you reason, self-control scrambling away faster than rats from a burning building.

When we act, say, go, or do what we shouldn't, we lose control—and end up regretting it. The Bible teaches that self-control and moderation is achievable. Our desires may tempt us, but they don't have to control us. Even while we're dieting!

Because we belong to the day, we must live decent lives for all to see. Don't participate in the darkness of wild parties and drunkenness, or in sexual promiscuity and immoral living, or in quarreling and jealousy. Instead, clothe yourself with the presence of the Lord Jesus Christ. And don't let yourself think about ways to indulge your evil desires.

ROMANS 13:13–14 NLT

Father, Your Holy Spirit is telling me that self-control is not one of my strengths and I need to work on it. I need temperance. Help me turn things over to You and allow You to develop self-control in my life. Amen.

And we are instructed to turn from godless living and sinful pleasures. We should live in this evil world with wisdom, righteousness, and devotion to God.

TITUS 2:12 NLT

Lord, keep me on the right path when my own plans are flawed, because only You know where You need me to be today and tomorrow. Amen.

Let your gentle spirit be known to all men. The Lord is near.
PHILIPPIANS 4:5 NASB

Father, help me show others my need for self-control, to not give in to the temptation of sin. Only when we turn from sin can we truly gain understanding in all wisdom. We ask for Your strength to help in this. Amen

For to this you were called, because Christ also suffered for us, leaving us an example, that you should follow His steps: "Who committed no sin, nor was deceit found in His mouth"; who, when He was reviled, did not revile in return; when He suffered, He did not threaten, but committed Himself to Him who judges righteously.

1 PETER 2:21–23 NKJV

Rules for proper behavior keep us from getting hurt. We risk our own life and the lives of others when we give in to our desires, whatever they might be.

LINDA BARTLETT

Sin

Some think that *sin* is too harsh a word. So they use euphemisms for sin such as mistake, blunder, fault, offense, or violation, which sound much better. We might try to whitewash it, but sin is just that—sin.

The scriptures define *sin* as knowing to do good but not doing it. No one is blameless. We have all sinned and are in need of repentance and forgiveness.

Jesus came to fix the sin problem. Just ask Him. He's not afraid of the word *sin*—He conquered it!

My little children, these things write I unto you, that ye sin not. And if any man sin, we have an advocate with the Father, Jesus Christ the righteous: And he is the propitiation for our sins: and not for ours only, but also for the sins of the whole world.

1 John 2:1–2 KJV

Father, every day is a battle. I struggle between following You and choosing what feels right at the moment. I need Your wisdom and power to persevere toward a true change of heart and action. But, most of all, I need Your forgiveness. Amen.

"Of Him all the prophets bear witness that through His name everyone who believes in Him receives forgiveness of sins."
ACTS 10:43 NASB

Father, I know it is Your will for me to understand Your Word, and You've given me the Holy Spirit to guide me. Help me to take advantage of this great blessing. Amen.

But if we walk in the Light as He Himself is in the Light, we have fellowship with one another, and the blood of Jesus His Son cleanses us from all sin.

1 JOHN 1:7 NASB

Lord, help me study Your Word and grow in knowledge of You in order to attain godliness. Then I can be an example to others of how to live godly lives. Amen.

But he was pierced for our rebellion, crushed for our sins. He was beaten so we could be whole. He was whipped so we could be healed. All of us, like sheep, have strayed away. We have left God's paths to follow our own. Yet the LORD laid on him the sins of us all.

ISAIAH 53:5–6 NLT

It is the very nature of sin to prevent man from meditating on spiritual things.

MARY MARTHA SHERWOOD

Sincerity

Sincerity is as welcoming as nestling in a cozy chair in front of a fire on a brisk, cold day.

The motives behind what we say or do are at the core of a sincere heart. Are our motives pure and genuine? Or do we possess a selfish, hidden agenda? Someone who demonstrates sincerity of heart and pure motives is a person whom we can trust.

Similarly, God expects us to approach Him in a straightforward manner with unadulterated sincerity. Hypocrisy has no place in our relationship with Him. God knows our heart and He seeks one seeped in sincerity.

So think clearly and exercise self-control. Look forward to the gracious salvation that will come to you when Jesus Christ is revealed to the world.

1 PETER 1:13 NLT

Father, I know that I tend to get focused on the negatives, and sometimes my thoughts are crowded with impatience, envy, anger, or resentment. Please help me focus on You. Fill me with pure thoughts. Amen.

For I say, through the grace given to me, to everyone who is among you, not to think of himself more highly than he ought to think, but to think soberly, as God has dealt to each one a measure of faith.

ROMANS 12:3 NKJV

Father, I know You blessed me abundantly in the family You have given me. Help me not to flaunt them or to take the credit that belongs to You. Amen.

We can say with confidence and a clear conscience that we have lived with a God-given holiness and sincerity in all our dealings. We have depended on God's grace, not on our own human wisdom. That is how we have conducted ourselves before the world, and especially toward you.

2 Corinthians 1:12 NLT

Lord, I ask for Your help in raising my children. May Your patience and kindness be made visible through my actions. Amen.

And in their mouth was found no deceit,
for they are without fault before the throne of God.
REVELATION 14:5 NKJV

Speaking beautifully is little to the purpose unless one lives beautifully.
ELIZABETH PRENTISS

Strength

Why do we wait until our strength is depleted before we seek God?

Women carry the weight of the world on their shoulders. We worry about our families as we manage our homes and assist our friends, churches, and communities. We maintain busy schedules as we transport kids to soccer practice and school functions. We cook, clean, work, and care for aging parents. No wonder we run out of steam!

Yet God wants us to rely upon His strength, not ours—to exchange our weakness for His power. What are you waiting for? Seek God's strength.

Wealth and honor come from you alone, for you rule over everything. Power and might are in your hand, and at your discretion people are made great and given strength.

1 Chronicles 29:12 NLT

Father God, though Your strength is limitless, it's tempered with wisdom and gentleness. You are both my strong tower and my tender, loving Father. Help me to find that proper balance of gentle strength in my own life. Amen.

"For the eyes of the LORD run to and fro throughout the whole earth, to show Himself strong on behalf of those whose heart is loyal to Him. In this you have done foolishly; therefore from now on you shall have wars."

2 CHRONICLES 16:9 NKJV

Make my heart perfect, Lord. Take my hand, and give me strength. Be strong for me when I don't measure up. My way to attain a perfect heart is through You, Lord, so don't take Your eyes off me. Amen.

That ye might walk worthy of the Lord unto all pleasing, being fruitful in every good work, and increasing in the knowledge of God; strengthened with all might, according to his glorious power, unto all patience and longsuffering with joyfulness.

COLOSSIANS 1:10–11 KJV

Because of Your strength, Lord,
I can smile. When I need peace,
You strengthen me on the inside.
This is where I need You the most.
Let me reflect Your strength so that
my children will be drawn to
You also. Amen.

Wait on the LORD; be of good courage, and He shall strengthen your heart; wait, I say, on the LORD!

PSALM 27:14 NKJV

We must continue to ask God for wisdom and insight and for the strength to persevere. He will cause us to rise up and fly like eagles, walking and not fainting.

NORMA SMALLEY

Temptation

Jesus fasted and prayed in the wilderness for forty days and the devil tempted Him, albeit unsuccessfully.

Our Savior faced temptation, and so do we. Although it presents itself in different forms, temptation is what Satan uses to defeat, discourage, and pollute the believer's mind and heart. He will use every nasty trick and deceptive device to get us to sin.

But don't worry. Martin Luther once said that we can't stop a bird from flying over our heads, but we can prevent it from building a nest there. Temptation will come—but it need not set up housekeeping.

"Watch and pray, lest you enter into temptation.
The spirit indeed is willing, but the flesh is weak."
MATTHEW 26:41 NKJV

Lord, I am human and often tempted. Be with me when I am tempted and show me the true joys of self-control. Amen.

"And do not lead us into temptation, but deliver us from evil. [For Yours is the kingdom and the power and the glory forever. Amen.]"

MATTHEW 6:13 NASB

Father, the life I am living right now is not the result of my faith in You but of Your faith in me. Thank You for Your sacrifice that saves me and makes me whole. Amen.

There hath no temptation taken you but such as is common to man: but God is faithful, who will not suffer you to be tempted above that ye are able; but will with the temptation also make a way to escape, that ye may be able to bear it.

1 Corinthians 10:13 KJV

Lord, the next time I am faced with danger for Your sake, let me remember that You are faithful to reward Your people, no matter how much I may fear. Amen.

Let no man say when he is tempted, I am tempted of God: for God cannot be tempted with evil, neither tempteth he any man.

JAMES 1:13 KJV

Temptations come,
as a general rule,
when they are sought.

MARGARET OLIPHANT

Truth

Your child gets in trouble at school. You question her, insisting on the whole truth. The doctor has bad news. You want the truth, despite your fear and hesitation.

In situations like these, truth becomes all-important. Yet truth is even more essential in our walk with God.

In the Bible, the idea of *truth* carries four interpretations: 1) actual, true to fact; 2) real, ideal, genuine; 3) dealing faithfully or truly with others; and 4) truth in all its fullness and scope, as embodied in Jesus, showing sincerity and integrity of character. To know Jesus is to know the truth.

These are the things you are to do: Speak the truth to each other, and render true and sound judgment in your courts.

ZECHARIAH 8:16 NIV

I'm ashamed to admit that I often speak before I think, and the words that come out of my mouth are not always truthful. Please help me be a good example. Amen.

"The Rock! His work is perfect, for all His ways are just; a God of faithfulness and without injustice, righteous and upright is He."
DEUTERONOMY 32:4 NASB

Father, help me to be diligent in understanding You and Your precepts. Please give me a continuous desire to know You better. Amen.

"And you shall know the truth, and the truth shall make you free."

JOHN 8:32 NKJV

Lord, let me know when I am wrong. That way I can come to You for cleansing and an opportunity to make things right. Thank You for the truth in Your Word, even though sometimes the truth hurts. Amen.

For their sakes I sanctify Myself, that they themselves also may be sanctified in truth.

John 17:19 NASB

If we are Christians, we have committed ourselves to the Lord Jesus Christ who said, "I am the Truth." In giving ourselves to Him, we dedicate ourselves to the truth not only about Him but about ourselves.

Pamela Hoover Heim

Understanding

Eleanor Roosevelt said, "Understanding is a two-way street." We'd all like to be understood, but do we understand? To gain understanding we must consider another's perspective apart from our own. In essence, we must walk in their shoes.

Knowing God gives us a greater appreciation for and understanding of others. As we view people and life through His eyes, our viewpoint changes. The things we once questioned, we now perceive with greater clarity and purpose.

To understand rather than to be understood is every Christian woman's quest for spiritual maturity. To understand while seldom understood is that quest realized.

Then shalt thou understand the fear of the LORD,
and find the knowledge of God. For the LORD giveth wisdom:
out of his mouth cometh knowledge and understanding.

PROVERBS 2:5–6 KJV

Father, I know my understanding is weak. But when I am in need of guidance, the first place I turn to is Your Word. Help me to search diligently, for I know the answers I need are there. Amen.

Therefore if there is any consolation in Christ, if any comfort of love, if any fellowship of the Spirit, if any affection and mercy, fulfill my joy by being like-minded, having the same love, being of one accord, of one mind.

PHILIPPIANS 2:1–2 NKJV

Lord, help me to be understanding with everyone I come into contact with, to encourage rather than discourage. I want to take their hands and walk with them, as You've taken time to walk with me. Amen.

When I was a child, I used to speak like a child, think like a child, reason like a child; when I became a man, I did away with childish things.

1 CORINTHIANS 13:11 NASB

Lord, I'm grateful that I have the opportunity to teach my children the truths that are found in Your Word. I'm trusting that You will open their spiritual understanding. I am looking forward to the day that they will accept You as Savior. Amen.

Make me understand the way of Your precepts;
so shall I meditate on Your wonderful works.
PSALM 119:27 NKJV

Yearn to understand first and
to be understood second.
BECA LEWIS ALLEN

Wisdom

According to Webster's dictionary, wisdom is "the power of judging correctly, following the soundest course of action based on knowledge, experience, understanding and good judgment."

God is wisdom personified. His wisdom far exceeds our most impressive reaches of thought. The scriptures explain that "the foolishness of God is wiser than men; and the weakness of God is stronger than men" (1 Corinthians 1:25 KJV). God alone is the source of true wisdom. Accordingly, we should seek His wisdom and discernment in every decision we make. To do so is just plain wise.

My son, pay attention to what I say; turn your ear to my words.
Do not let them out of your sight, keep them within your heart;
for they are life to those who find them and health to one's whole body.

PROVERBS 4:20–22 NIV

Lord, I need Your gentle wisdom for every area of life. I'm so thankful that what You offer is the best. Amen.

But if any of you lacks wisdom, let him ask of God, who gives to all generously and without reproach, and it will be given to him.

JAMES 1:5 NASB

Father, please give me the wisdom I need to properly advise my children. Help me teach them to seek guidance from Your Word and in communion with the Holy Spirit. Amen.

I will instruct thee and teach thee in the way which thou shalt go: I will guide thee with mine eye.

PSALM 32:8 KJV

Lord, help me realize that my understanding is not necessary for the completion of Your plan. You understand everything; all I need to do is have faith. Amen.

For wisdom is protection just as money is protection,
but the advantage of knowledge is that wisdom
preserves the lives of its possessors.
ECCLESIASTES 7:12 NASB

Learning is not attained by chance, it must be sought for with ardor and attended to with diligence.
ABIGAIL ADAMS